THE JOKE BOOK

Robots: The Joke Book
First published in the USA by HarperKids Entertainment in 2005
First published in Great Britain by HarperCollinsEntertainment 2005
HarperCollinsEntertainment is an imprint of HarperCollins Publishers Ltd,
77-85 Fulham Palace Road, Hammersmith, London W6 8JB

Typography by Rick Farley
www.robotsmovie.com
www.harpercollinschildrensbooks.co.uk

ISBN 0-00-719223-1

1 2 3 4 5 6 7 8 9 10

ROBOTS™

THE JOKE BOOK

Written by Megan Howard
and
Jedidiah Fretts Howard

HarperCollins*Entertainment*
An imprint of HarperCollinsPublishers

Rodney Copperbottom: Why did the robot love the movie *Robots*?

Fender: Because it was *rivet*ing.

Nuts and bolts

Rodney: What does a frightened robot do when he is in danger?

Bigweld: He bolts.

Mr. Copperbottom: Why couldn't the robot sleep?

Mrs. Copperbottom: He was wired.

Crank Casey: How do you annoy a robot?

Lug: Push his buttons.

Rodney: Why did the robot run away?

Fender: He wanted to join the circuits.

Rodney: Why did the hungry robot log on to the computer?

Fender: Because he wanted some chips.

Lug: What's a robot's favorite snack?

Crank: Nuts.

Rodney: Did you hear the joke about the dishwasher bot and the vacuum cleaner bot?

Cappy: Yes, it was very clean.

Bigweld: What did Piper Pinwheeler say to the Rusties when they were about to battle Ratchet?

Fender: Let's go kick some ro-butt!

Rodney: Hey, dad, how does a robot shave?

Mr. Copperbottom: With a *laser* blade, of course!

DID YOU STEEL THAT?

Piper Pinwheeler: What do you call a cowboy bot?

Fender: *Chrome* on the range.

Ratchet: Did you hear about the sale on spare parts?

Madame Gasket: Yes, they're a *steel*.

Mr. Copperbottom: Which robots are the healthiest?

Mrs. Copperbottom: The ones who get enough iron.

Rodney: Why was the robot so annoying?

Cappy: He was always *metal*ing in other robots's business.

KNOCKS AND PINGS

Rodney: Knock, knock.

Cappy: Who's there?

Rodney: A bottle.

Cappy: A bottle who?

Rodney: A bot'll get the job done.

Lug: Knock, knock.

Crank: Who's there?

Lug: Juno.

Crank: Juno who?

**Lug: Juno know
I'm a robot?**

Piper: Knock, knock.

Fender: Who's there?

Piper: Iron.

Fender: Iron who?

**Piper: Iron an allowance
every week.**

Bigweld: Knock, knock.

Ratchet: Who's there?

Bigweld: Weld.

Ratchet: Weld who?

Bigweld: Weld, you'll find out if you open the door.

Madame Gasket: Knock, knock.

Ratchet: Who's there?

Madame Gasket: Wire.

Ratchet: Wire who?

Madame Gasket: Wire you so nosy?

**Mr. Copperbottom:
Knock, knock.**

Mrs. Copperbottom:
Who's there?

**Mr. Copperbottom:
Dishwasher.**

Mrs. Copperbottom:
Dishwasher who?

**Mr. Copperbottom: Dishwasher way
I talked before I got my teeth fixed.**

Fender: Knock, knock.

Piper: Who's there?

Fender: Fender.

Piper: Fender who?

Fender: Please 'fend her. She's in trouble!

Leadbetter: Knock, knock.

Forge: Who's there?

Leadbetter: Leadbetter.

Forge: Leadbetter who?

Leadbetter: Leadbetter not rust.

Forge: Knock, knock.

Leadbetter: Who's there?

Forge: Forge.

Leadbetter: Forge who?

Forge: Forge jokes are better than one.

OUTMODES

Lug: Why did the robot cross the busy highway?

Crank: Because she was nuts.

Lug: No, no. That's not right. Why did the robot cross the busy highway?

Crank: Because she had a screw loose.

Rodney: You're driving the train from Rivet Town to Robot City.

Fender: Okay.

Rodney: At the first stop, three robots get on, and none get off. At the second stop, eight robots get on, and two get off. At the third stop, five robots get on, and eight get off.

Fender: Got it.

Rodney: What color are the train driver's eyes?

Fender: Huh? How would I know?

Rodney: Same as yours. I said, "*You're* driving the train."

Cappy: Why did the robot cross the road?

Rodney: Why?

Cappy: To get *USA Today*. Do you get it?

Rodney: No.

Cappy: Neither do I. I get the *Robot City News*.

Bigweld: Did you hear about the robot that was built upside down?

Aunt Fan: Yes, his feet smelled and his nose ran.

Cappy: What happened when the robot sprang a leak in her sleep?

Piper: She woke up *oily* the next morning.

Leadbetter: What time is it when three robots chase you?

Forge: Three after one.

Out of this world

Rodney: What do you call a robot that does yoga?

Cappy: A *bending* machine.

Piper: Why did the failing robot study for her test?

Fender: She needed an *upgrade*.

Crank: Did you hear the one about the stinky welder bot?

Lug: Yes, he *smelt* up the place.

Cappy: What do you call a robot sailor?

Aunt Fan: A *row*-bot.

TECH TALK

What does a frog robot say?

"Rivet rivet."

How do you greet a robot repairman?

"Hi, tech!"

How do you greet a three-headed robot?

"Hello. Hello. Hello."

What did the robot child say to her angry parents?

"It's not my fault. I'm just a kit."

ROBOT RAVES

What's a robot's favorite . . .

. . . sport?

Gasketball.

. . . game?

Robotic-tac-toe.

. . . drink?

Dr. Piper.

. . . country?

Grease.

. . . season?

Spring.

. . . superhero?

Superman, the Man
of Steel.

. . . cartoon?

*SpongeBot
SpareParts.*

. . . movie?

*The Lizzie McWire
Movie.*

. . . rerun?

*Sabrina, the
Teenage Widget.*

. . . sitcom?

Malcolm in the Metal.

. . . music?

Heavy metal.

. . . song?

"Row, Row, Row Your Bot."

. . . dance?

The robot, of course.

. . . female pop singer?

Britney Gears.

. . . boy band?

'Nzinc.

. . . member of a boy band?

Just-Tin Timberlake.

COPPERBOTTOM CRACK-UPS

What makes a Copperbottom shine?

A little elbow grease.

What do you get when you cross a dishwasher bot with an angry giant frog?

A mean, green cleaning machine.

What do you get when you cross Rodney with a canary?

A robot that sings.

What's the difference between Rodney Copperbottom and an exhaust fan?

One invents, the other vents out.

Why was Cappy attracted to Rodney?

He had a magnetic personality.

Rusty Parts

Fender: What's it called when Aunt Fan bumps into me?

Rodney: I don't know, what?

**Fender:
A Fender bender.**

Rodney: Did you hear the one about Aunt Fan?

Bigweld: Yes, it has a huge ending.

Why do the Rusties love their home?

It belongs to their biggest Fan.

Why did Fender's head fall off?

It wasn't attached to his ro-body.

Why did Fender lose his mind?

He had a screw loose.

How are Fender and Piper related?

He's her *bro*bot and she's his tran*sis*tor.

What happened when Piper got her wires crossed?

She was a twisted sister.

What do you call a grumpy robot?

Crank.

What do you call a robot carrying a heavy bag?

Lug.

Where does Lug sit when he goes to a movie?

Anywhere he wants.

What's the difference between a silent Rusty and a rodent who doesn't bathe?

One's a wordless diesel, the other's a dirty weasel.

What do you get when you cross an outmode and some bread?

A crusty Rusty.

What time is it when Aunt Fan, Lug, and Bigweld sit on a bench?

Time to get a new bench.

Bigweld
Big Shots

What do you call the executives at Bigweld Industries?

The top brass.

What's the difference between a nervous Bigweld Industries executive and a baby?

One is a Leadbetter, the other is a bed wetter.

Where does Bigweld go to the bathroom?

In the executive *rust*room.

Why did they rush Bigweld to the hospital?

He was in cardiac a-*rust*.

What do you call a Bigweld executive bot who's in a good mood?

A happy Cappy.

What do you call a Bigweld executive bot who dresses nicely?

A snappy Cappy.

What do you get when you cross the greatest robot in the world with a sphere?

A Bigweld Ball.

Ratchet Up

First minion: What do you get when you cross a canary with Madame Gasket?

Second minion: Nothing. You *don't* cross Madame Gasket!

Why did the robot end up in the Chop Shop?

He was really just nuts.

What does Ratchet call pure evil?

"Mom."

Why did Madame Gasket polish Ratchet?

She wanted to see her son shine.

What's the difference between Madame Gasket's underlings and killer scallions?

One group is evil minions, the other is evil onions.

What's Madame Gasket's favorite dessert?

Pie à la *out*mode.

What happens when Ratchet has a bad hair day?

He keeps forgetting his point.

Why did Ratchet shock so many robots?

He was a high-powered executive.

What do you get when you cross a spy bot with a machine that rounds up outmodes?

A sweeper peeper.

What's on Madame Gasket's tombstone?

Rust in peace.

Tongue Twisters

Try saying these ten times fast:

Greedy Gasket grabs go guys.

Sisters shine.

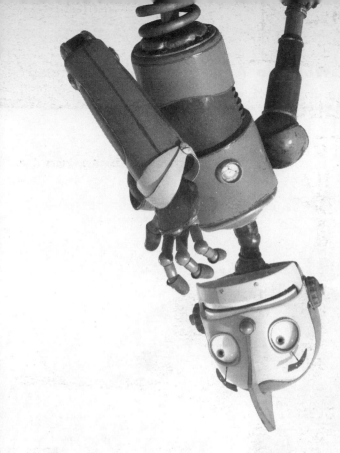

Aunt Fan's fanny frightened Fender's friend.

Fender and his friends fight Madame's measly minions.

Really rusty robots rule the rain.

Rodney: What do Aunt Fan's backside and this page have in common?

Fender: The big ending.